I0109026

No Longer Gravity's Partner

Poems by

JP DiBlasi

BLUE LIGHT PRESS ◆ 1ST WORLD PUBLISHING

1ST WORLD
PUBLISHING

SAN FRANCISCO ◆ FAIRFIELD ◆ DELHI

No Longer Gravity's Partner

Copyright ©2019 by JP DiBlasi

All rights reserved. Printed in the United States of America. No part of this book may be used or reproduced in any manner whatsoever without written permission except in the case of brief quotations embodied in critical articles and reviews. For information contact:

1st World Library
PO Box 2211
Fairfield, IA 52556
www.1stworldpublishing.com

Blue Light Press
www.bluelightpress.com
bluelightpress@aol.com

Book & Cover Art & Design
Melanie Gendron
melaniegendron999@gmail.com

Author Photo
JP DiBlasi

First Edition

ISBN 978-1-4218-3820-5

No Longer Gravity's Partner

Contents

The Weaver

Spin spirals of silk ribbon
far across the frozen galaxy
gathering arpeggios of celestial light,
golden down of angel wings,
silent base notes of the nebula.

Weave this radiance into tapestry
embroidered with clusters of
white and dark stars,
luminous crystalline ice,
the canticles of cherubim.

Swaddle the galaxy
until it throbs and heaves
with the rhythm of love.

Illuminate those still-nameless corners
with phosphorescent threads,
magenta light, those faraway places
that sleep light years beyond
the crag of our moon.

April

"These are the high holy days of spring"
— Diane Porter

Sacramental waters swell narrow streams,
roil river rocks
through fissures cut by glaciers.

Brookies leap from liquid cold,
anointed now with names, fanning fins
and tails in liquid absolution.

Rainbows blush red,
translucent in silver radiance.

A doe and fawn
approach a mirrored pool
in the arm of a bend.
The little one sips the shine.

The mother watches,
catching their reflections in the inverse sky.

Oneness

*"The light that you see by is the light
that comes from inside."* — Radiance Sutras

Look closely.
Dark against light.

Shadow illuminates light,
lets you see everything, inside out.

The light of soul
endless fractals of spirit.

We're blind to light
without seeing shadow.

Mine and yours —
strange attractors.

The Uninvited Moon

The pond radiates the moon's
knife-edge fullness
across black satin skin.

There is no love between
introverted water
and the silver-blood eye
piercing the dark,

searing sleeping hives
of dreams, smoldering knots
of earth's black fire,
embryos of innocence.

At The Border

Between San Diego and Tijuana

On the beach,
where the forecast says blue skies.

Where the terns and plovers
scuttle sand, dance the onshore breeze.

We'll meet beyond the dunes,
along no garden's iron fence,
where the hawk gliding low
studs the air.

No gate to let us in.

I'll bring you pictures. See how tall
she's grown, in her big girl dress?
You'll tell me about my brother,
Mamá and young José.

We'll press our faces to the mesh,
cry burning tears,
small pinky fingers
the only things that kiss.

First Person Elephant

Based on an Exhibition at the Elephant Hotel
Somers, NY Historical Society

We walked under a moonless sky.
Nothing was familiar: the position of stars,
the smell of dry earth, whip-poor-will calls
from strange night birds.

Absent were the sacred sounds
of evening ragas, the distant glimmer of lanterns.

The road was packed hard,
rutted by iron wheels of wagons
hauling seeds, milled flour, spun cotton cloth
on this north-south route.

Drovers lined us up.
We towered over them,
I was first, two camels behind me.

While everyone slept we became
the morning's surprise, a menagerie:
leathery ears, hairy necks
and a trunk that could reach into trees,
a fiery mane, a black tufted tail.

One elephant, two camels,
a lion in a cage.

I bow to your species.
I never knew your names.

Au Nom de Père

Death again, in god's name.

Media doesn't show the faces
of the newly dead,
too quickly converted into data anonymity:
numbers lost, attack locations,
three at the stadium, four in restaurants,
the deadliest, a concert at the Bataclan.

Suddenly, when the bombs exploded
and the world tilted upside down,
I saw everything through the eyes of the dead.

In the grief of Paris, I recalled those who fell
or fled from towers in New York,
those eyes, brown and blue,
returning to me in my dreams.

Connecticut: Missing Boy

For David

They searched the Housatonic:
the town rescue squad,
friends,
kayakers,
your father.

No one wanted to find you
lying still beneath the falls,
pulled under by the swollen
raging waters.

They walked the river banks
with ropes and poles,
searched downstream hoping
to find you lying on an outcropping of rocks,
or draped over a limb
just before the bend in the river,
dazed.

You were everyone's son
those June days
lengthened with light,
shortened by despair.

Red Bird

"Today sky and earth are steeped in gray and soaked in mist.
It's nice seeing this male Northern Cardinal /make a point of
bright." — Diane Porter

The mist of morning
washed corridors of gray
into late afternoon,
lifting deep stains of darkness
from the night before.

At the bell for evening hours,
a cardinal rose from the Tamarack,
and with the muscle of its wings
anointed the gray, forgiving it with color
from the setting sun.

Garden Rosary

I water the plants in my garden
by the Hail Mary, not by the
gallon, quart or pint.
Not by the raised markings
on the watering can,
nor by runoff over edges
of red clay or wood box containers.

Each basket of full-faced fireball marigolds
showered with half a Hail Mary.

Urns of black magic,
petunias are graced
with the Rosary,
the Our Father and Glory Be.
The crescendo of daylilies
near the stone wall, are bathed in a cascade,
twenty-four petitions,
for another summer filled with blossoms.

Last spring during the drought,
I offered Aves to the lilacs
using captured winter run-off
and recycled rinse water

I never thought about prayer
but it is, of course, what we do
when we're frightened or worried.

We pray,
name by name
one silent bead at a time.

Sister Said

St. Joseph's School

"And now, girls and boys, we will read aloud
about the life of a favorite saint."

*But I don't want to read aloud about a favorite
Saint. I want to read about the Mohicans
and how they made birch bark canoes.*

"And what saint should we read about," Sister asked?
"St. Lucy," Clare replied.
"St. Peter," said Kathleen.

Next time, girls.
"Today, I've selected St. Ann," Sister said.

Not St. Ann, again. I cringed, with bleak despair.

"Before we read the story of St. Ann,"
Sister said, "let's all say one Hail Mary
to clear our minds."

Not my mind. I thought, running to the edge.
I want to jump in that birch bark canoe,
push out into the Hudson, dip my paddle
into endless hidden passages of watery time.

I want to listen to it whisper as it laps
the sides of the thin bark skin. I want to see the
Red-tail fly, spot its nest on the Palisades,
find the wind-worn faces of the ancestors
in the cloud streaked sky.

I felt Sister near, yet far away, talking,
talking about something I couldn't really hear.
She tapped my canoe with her finger.
"And you, you, what did you like best
about the life of St. Ann?"

I looked heavenward, saw the Red-tail smile.
"Well, Sister," said I, "the thing I liked best
was the Hail Mary. It settled my mind,
just as you said it would."

Casting the Moon Shot

Calling all moons:
blue moons, silver moons,
bad moons rising.

Crescent moons, full moons,
moons from Mars.
Killing moons, hungry moons,
moons with dark sides and shadows,
waxing, waning, draped in gauzy ghosts.

Gather tomorrow, dusk to dawn,
to launch a paper moon
sailing over a cardboard sea.

Love on the N Train

They're seated on the N train.
Young women snapping gum,
reading dog-eared paperbacks,
love tales, *Fifty Shades of Grey*,
looking for Mr. Right.

Young men, styling gold chains and
after shave, looking at girls,
side glances, pausing
at breasts, ankles, knees.

Everyone's looking for love, reading
about love, listening to songs about love.
Even the homeless man slumped across
two corner seats at the end of the car
dreams about love.

The N stops at Queensboro Plaza.
People with shopping bags and backpacks
rustle on and off. Some run for the doors,
others for newly emptied seats. Books slip
from backpacks, as the homeless man sleeps.

A young man sits next to me, music spilling
from ear buds. He moves rhythmically,
softly, keeping time.
His knee brushes mine.

By 57th Street I've danced with everyone
I can ever remember dancing with — at the prom,
strangers at the Fire Island Pines, surviving with Donna
Summers in the disco, the music vibrating in my chest,

the deaf DJ crankin' them out. Dancing with men,
dancing with women, in small groups and alone.

Then, I remembered the way you held me,
felt your right hand in the small of my back,
your knee leaning into mine. We slow danced
for an eternity, long after the music stopped.

Pencils

I love pencils
the way they rest
cradled by the thumb
in the fingers of my speechless hand.

I love the way they feel:
firm,
round,
hexagonal.

I love the Dixon Ticonderoga
Faber Castell
American Eagle,
but especially the Venus Velvet
No. 2's of my childhood.

I love the way they nuzzle
the fibers of the page,
the sounds they make
carving letters onto paper
giving voice to words coaxed
from mind to nerve to muscle
through arm & hand & fingers.

I love the deliberate sounds,
staccato, crossing t's,
etching capital letters,
thrusting downward strokes of l's
for life & love & lavender.

I love the soft gray trail
of graphite revealing inner thoughts
of mind & soul
the way they sing & cry, ponder & poke
& sometimes spell things out
in ways I had not intended.

Standing on Third

> "We have no tickets back to our childhood."
> — Mary Mackey

I hear the crack of the bat,
the ump calling *play ball.*
I'm on the edge,
mitt in hand, eyes on the wind-up
as the ball rolls off the pitcher's knuckles
dancing a tango toward home.

The batter misses, swinging at air.
Groans and cheers swell
as men hawk *beer here, beer here*
and the organ drones *do, re, mi*
sustaining the *mi* to fire-up fan fever.

So very unlike the organ at church

where I sit on the girls' side, missal open
to Latin responses intoned
after invocations from the priest.
No music invites excitement down these aisles,
only a solitary, hands folded, eyes down shuffle
of solemnity every Sunday at nine.

As a child, I always wondered why this was.

Now that I've tripled to third, eye-level with the pitch,
the three notes from the ball park organ ring in my ears
as I pray the next batter-up hammers the light,
sending me home.

It's Existential

In my dream
someone I don't recognize
is reading my mind,
one word at a time.

Or perhaps they're writing
in cursive, composing
my dream.

I can't tell.

I don't recognize the hand
but the touch feels familiar.
Could be my own,
or maybe even yours?

I feel the touch each letter makes,
the curl of the C,
the carve of the X,
the scribble of the looping capital M.

Am I living the dream
or is the dream living me?
It doesn't matter.
Save me a seat.

What the Eyes Say

Kaleidoscope eyes,
eyes wide shut,
more than meets the eyes,
psychoanalyze.

Piercing eyes,
puppy dog eyes,
old blue eyes that
hypnotize.

Blind eyes,
snake eyes,
lying eyes,
jeopardize.

Jaundice eyes,
wandering eyes,
pie-eyed eyes,
alibis.

Bedroom eyes,
goo goo eyes,
come hither eyes,
eroticize.

The Margins

We love at the margins.
A golden arc,
the scent of heat and light
between us. A crystal hue
illuminates dark passageways.

We shimmer
wrapped in deep surrender
together and alone
under a half lit moon,
a tangle of tongues
in the grasp of a knot.

Darkness

speaks the poetry of shadows.
Silent silhouettes slither
across the unlit back room wall,
snuggle into corners under a blue-black
veil of mystery.

Darkness, a lived-in place,
ebony-infused, mahogany highlights,
hints of black raspberries,
the wine we drank that last evening.

I stare at the wall, silently reading
the shadows, reaching for transparent
images, listening, hoping
I will recognize you.

Adoration

You are the ruby
woven into velvet robes,
the ermine and silk
adornment of scarves,
the breath of gossamer wind
spun into the pleated blouse.
I am the tailor.

You are the creamy luster of pearls,
the shimmer of cut diamonds,
the seduction of gold strands
and rings of sky sapphire.
I am the jeweler.

All else, plain cloth
and dust.
I am poor hands.

Blackbird

Deep in the forest at the end of the world,
a silken place not shackled by the moon,
a blackbird sings a liquid scale
of shooting stars.

Here, all light has been absorbed.
The audience of deciduous trees
casts no shadows.
The blackbird's yellow beak
and eye rings
darkened in its feathered form

where color is illuminated
on the inside,
where winged birdsong
arcs in the key of blue heat.

Still Life

Reflection on the river ignites blue,
with cumulus clouds, mirror images,
a reverse painting on glass.

I cast no shadow.
No solitary peregrine rides the updrafts,
no sails beat leeward, no breeze whispers,
only your breath upon my cheek.

The tide is hushed.
No currents of tongues lap the banks.
I'm drawn to the edge,
where the fish at my feet
are stars waiting to sing.

Sancta Communio

I am the supplicant
at the rail of morning's breath,
the moment the body and blood of darkness
casts shadows
against awakening light,
until darkness is only shadow
breathed by light
and I drink from the cup of
consecrated sky.

Recurring Dream

It's always the same:
the awakening of night,
first light before the trillium and tiger lilies,
the muffle of the white bird's wings
at my face as she silently lifts
the corner of my patchless quilt
and lays it like a silken mantel on my shoulders.

The Falls

Salisbury, Connecticut

Silent,
crystal stalactites
rouged by the setting sun.
Pine shadows stretch across
the river's bend, slowly extinguishing
the slender birch's silver blaze.

I see them through winter's branches
speechless without their leaves,
listening for what they might whisper.

I imagine you cold, below the icy silence,
remember when the river, surging
after long rains, claimed you
that warm June day the school year ended.

Every time I pass,
I hear your voice
chanting the cold river's
requiem.

In Memory of KP

No Longer Gravity's Partner

"...you really are a golden bird that needs to dance."
— Hafiz

You are flying
beyond the zenith
of hawks and doves,
dancing star to star,
moon to moon,
solo through illuminated darkness,
silk labyrinths of light,
shimmering oms,
temple bells
on weightless golden wings.

For Margie, Mary and BJ

About the Author

JP DiBlasi is a native New Yorker currently living and writing in the Hudson River town of Ossining. "Au Nom de Pere" was published in *Carrying The Branch: Poets in Search of Peace*, (Glass Lyre Press, 2017). Her poems have also been published in *Chronogram*, *Poetry Breakfast*, and *RiverRiver*. She is interested in traditional Irish music, attends local music sessions and teaches the bodhrán, the Irish goat skin drum. Friends love her sense of humor.

www.ingramcontent.com/pod-product-compliance
Lightning Source LLC
Chambersburg PA
CBHW021917040426
42447CB00007B/899